# The Good Side of a Bad Man

billy the kid

# The Good Side

# of a Bad Man

by

Lee Priestley

with

Marquita Peterson

*Illustrated by Marquita Peterson*

*Yucca Tree Press*

Revised Printing      1993

Cover design: Block print by Marquita Peterson

Library of Congress Cataloging in Publication Data.

Priestley, Lee, and Marquita Peterson

Billy the Kid: The Good Side of a Bad Man
   1. William Bonney. 2. Billy the Kid.
   3. Outlaws - Southwest. 3. Southwest United States - History.
   I. Lee Priestley. II. Marquita Peterson. III. Title.

Library of Congress Catalog Card Number: 93-061580

ISBN: 1-881325-10-5

# CONTENTS

# WANTED

## INFORMATION

## REGARDING

## "THE GOOD SIDE OF A BAD MAN"

# BILLY THE KID

LEE PRIESTLEY - WRITER
MARQUITA PETERSON - ARTIST
426 MIRANDA
LAS CRUCES, NM 88001

# The Case for the Defense

*Lo que no se empieza no se termina.*
What is not begun is never finished.

A writer and an artist, who were comparing notes from their travels away from the Land of Enchantment, were mutually surprised to learn that one New Mexican was internationally known, when more worthy contemporaries' very names were lost in dusty time. Even the citizens of sister states, who tend to believe that present-day New Mexicans live in a foreign country, knew of this infamous citizen!

Why? Why is the slight smiling youngster who lived at odds with the law and died at its hands more than a hundred years ago the lone New Mexican whose life is remembered halfway around the world?

William Bonney, a.k.a. Billy the Kid, has become a legend. Why else is he celebrated in dime (and more distinguished) novels, poems, songs, plays, ballets, festivals, pageants, seemingly endless movies and tourists' T-shirts? The media keeps his memory green with frequent speculation about his life and death—or even whether he died. Fan clubs proliferate; tourism promoters get into the action. Museums and officials vie for the ownership and right to exhibit small personal properties. Clearly, New Mexico's best known citizen is a tourist attraction second only to Carlsbad Caverns.

When the artist studied one of the few pictures of the Kid, instead of the usual much retouched image of a slack-jawed boy staring vacantly, she saw a sly, smiling show-off, little different from a teenager of today. The writer, slogging through pounds of print, found references and quotes that summed up the Kid as "a pretty good boy and better than most."

It all suggested that Billy the Kid was no ordinary bad man. Certainly he was no angel, but angels were in short supply in New Mexico Territory during the 1870s and 1880s. Then, the prevalent lawlessness was more a matter of disorder than immorality. Life was hard and the first imperative was survival. Billy, survived as did many others, and largely by the same means. Much depended upon who enforced the law. The ranchers and settlers played deadly games with both sides of the law, each using different rule books.

No one denies that William Bonney lived outside the law. He stole horses. He rustled cattle. He killed a few citizens, but not, the evidence declares, the "twenty-one, one for each year of his life," he is charged with. He died as violently as he had lived. But so did many others of his day. Why are they forgotten while he is remembered? Why has he become a legend? Under the overlay of time, what was he really like?

Would it be possible to find him, not as he as seen by writers of the time —who were often motivated to overlook, if not suppress, any favorable side —but see him as he appeared to the seldom quoted folk who knew him most intimately? What about the viewpoints and opinions that never made it into print? How did the small ranchers and farmers and villagers see him? The two friends thought of a way to find out.

The artist prepared an "Information Wanted" poster, picturing the Kid as her artist's eye saw him. The writer typed a news release that asked descendants of family and friends who had known New Mexico's number one citizen to share some of their memories. The two sent mailings to newspapers in the areas where the Kid had spent his short life. By searching for the genesis of the legend, it might be possible to understand why the Kid has such a firm hold on the interest of later generations.

The response was impressive. Letters came and have continued to come from addresses all over New Mexico and from other states as well. Many of the letters are in the shaky handwriting of old age; others are reminiscences told to young relatives and friends. Amateur and professional historians told of their belief that Billy had been a convenient scapegoat. Altogether, they spoke loudly for the defense.

"It's about time!" they wrote. "Time for the whole story to be told."

The hard economic facts of territorial life, and even some skeletons escaped from respectable closets, can be found in the handed-down recollections of people who actually knew the Kid. The writer and artist claim no spectacular discoveries. The story has always been there, buried under published strata of verifiable facts, half-truths and "downright lies." (Some of the writers used a more emphatic adjective.)

For every primary source that led to published material, other stories are related by those who shied away from being pinned down to the printed page. The kind of information the writer and the artist wanted had been kept out of written records.

To talk to anyone, but one's trusted friends, was once dangerous. Old timers, garrulous though they may seem, think long

3

and hard before they talk to strangers. Even when no one is left who might be hurt, they may not tell all they know. Historians must remember that it is impossible to "tell the truth, the whole truth and nothing but the truth" from the distance of a hundred years. It is inescapable that history changes with the telling. Like the people who have contributed to the printed pages, the letter writers can be prejudiced, or mistaken, or confused. The reader can only listen and believe as he can.

The letters that helped to show the good side of a man labeled by history as bad could be annotated and attributed, but the letter writers did not seem to want that. There were in the past, and still are, legitimate reasons for their reluctance. The violence and bloodshed of the turbulent territorial times left many scars, some of them on flinching flesh. More, less painful memories, are handed down in family annals. Although it may not be dangerous or unwise after a hundred years to air disagreements with neighbors, to do so doesn't make for amiable relationships, even now.

Another reason for not wanting to be tied to names, places and dates is fallible memory. Here are the recollections of old folks often unschooled except in the hard terms of life. They don't wish to court ridicule if their stories don't quite agree with those of published "book-learned" authors. But they "know what they know" and are vehement in their knowledge.

The writers compared Billy the Kid with military, commercial and political figures of the time—most often to Billy's advantage. He was simply, they felt, a boy of his times and circumstances, not worse than many and better than most. They didn't deny that he took a casual attitude toward property, especially if it were four-legged and portable, but so, they declared, did many, if not most, of his fellow Territorians. "Actually, no one really knew who the stock belonged to in the first place!"

They conceded that the Kid shot a few men in the course of his career, but they indignantly repudiated the "lies of the dime novel writers that he killed twenty-one men, not counting Indians and Mexicans." The number was more like seven or eight, they wrote. "Some of that number were shot in self-defense and the others needed killing."

With the letters providing the leads, the writer and the artist went interviewing. The tapes and notes grew and grew again; and the letters are still coming. So are the generous additions of those who wished to confirm the story. Obviously there are many gaps in the record of the Kid's life journey. "Of course, we don't know it all," they admit, "but neither did those writer fellers!" They tend to shy away from the minutely researched areas such as the Lincoln County War, but fierce partisans that they are, they feel free to doubt "some of the so-called facts."

In the beginning, an effort was made to verify everything and to give individual credit in footnotes. "No, no," they wrote. "We don't want that. Just tell the other side of the story."

That is what the writer and the artist have attempted to do. Take their word for it; the letters and notes and tapes exist. Anyone who wishes may read it all in our chaotic files. From that source material, here is testimony that attempts to show the good side of one who was both a victim of circumstances and a man of his time.

# Chapter One

*Le que bien se aprende tarde se olvida.*
What is well learned is not soon forgotten.

The boy knew better. Certainly. He could read the sign, *No trespassing! Trespassers will be prosecuted!* But the door of the shed stood ajar. The other kids had never seen anyone near and likely there was nothing but junk inside.

The junk was there all right, but the shed held something more intriguing. The boy pushed and pulled until a big, dome-topped trunk burst from a shower of dead leaves and lumber scraps. With a quick tug he broke the lock and lifted the lid. The boy's eyes widened and his grin spread at what he saw . . . .

Later that morning Silver City's Sheriff Whitehill, coming out of a cafe after his second cup of coffee, heard a commotion along Bullard Street. A strange girl, wearing a plumed hat too wide to go through a door, was tottering down the street on high heels, trailing long skirts held above red stockings. The girl pranced and wiggled until the ruffles behind shook lewdly.

With every wiggle and prance, the trail of kids and loafers grew longer and louder. The sheriff strode sternly to meet the ruckus. That girl might be the new one expected at the house on Chihuahua Hill, but she couldn't be allowed to advertise so openly!

'She' made a sweeping bow to the sheriff — and 'her' hat fell off. It was that kid again! This was once too much. The sheriff grabbed an ear and marched Henry Antrim (later known as William Bonney and The Kid) home to his mother, Catherine.

The letter writers offered several versions of what came next, but they agreed that the boy got into no more serious scrapes than did most poorly supervised youngsters. One writer excused the boy's early brushes with the law saying, "that he showed off, lied, swore, played cards and broke the Sabbath only proved that average orneriness was in him." Another commented, "He was about the same as most boys of his age."

His early years were filled with high spirits and minor conflicts with the law and the school system. Stories recalled by schoolmates were more laughable than serious. Those in Silver City remembered that he sang and danced and clowned in any available 'show.' He must have been good at those amateur theatricals for he had parts in the plays given at Morill's Opera House.

Showing off in class led to some troubles. His teacher, Miss Mary Roberts, once told him to "Sit down and shut up!" When his failure to be quiet brought her down the aisle, Billy ran for the door and there they met. As the teacher struggled to hold the wiggling boy, they both lost their balance and ended up on the floor. Miss Roberts was a large young woman, so she simply

10

sat on the boy to hold him down while whacking the part of his anatomy best suited to the purpose. It was so ridiculous they both shouted with laughter as the teacher landed each swat. Billy could always take a joke on himself.

When he settled down, he was a good student, learning easily and well. His handwriting became unusually clear, as the letters he much later exchanged with Governor Lew Wallace show. He became a reader, for he always requested reading material when he was jailed. In hiding at various times and places, he wanted newspapers as much as food and drink.

In the booming mining town, rough characters and questionable surroundings were more available than Sunday Schools and churches, but the boy was quoted later as saying that he went to church with his mother when she felt well enough to go. During the time of the Lincoln County War, he showed his familiarity with hymns and church music that both surprised and pleased three ladies who agreed that he hadn't acquired that knowledge at gaming tables or in saloons.

But Sheriff Whitehill was disappointed that taking Billy home to his mother hadn't produced much change. Catherine Antrim, only months away from her death, showed the same lightheartedness that characterized her son. Full of Irish wit and laughter, despite her tubercular frailness, she had excused her son and promised to keep him on a tighter rein.

The rein wasn't tight enough, for Billy came to the sheriff's attention again, this time accused of raiding the clothesline at the Chinese laundry. The long suffering owner, bedeviled by half the town, had complained to the sheriff, blaming Billy. Two writers believed an older boy had left Billy holding the sack, or more exactly, the shirts.

Sheriff Whitehill thought the boy wasn't really bad. He decided that a day or two in jail might teach him a lesson. So he locked Billy up.

Understandably, Billy didn't like the jail. The small dark room, five steps across and seven lengthwise, was lit only by what sunshine or moon glow could find the opening of the small, barred window. Staying there was real punishment. The letter writers disagreed about what came next. The sheriff, himself, told years later that the boy squeezed himself up and out of the narrow chimney. Another story teller recalled that the boy begged for exercise and was allowed the freedom of the hall. Then he simply walked away. Both stories are probably true for the sheriff had more than one exasperating contact with the boy.

After his mother's death, the boy, with his older brother Joe, went first to live with the Truesdell family. The boys worked for board and room by washing dishes and waiting tables at the hotel operated by Mr. Truesdell. Billy seemed to have been a more than satisfactory employee. "Henry was the only kid who worked at the hotel who didn't steal the silverware," said the hotel owner. "He was dependable."

William Antrim, the boys' stepfather, tried to care for the brothers by giving up work at the mines for a job in Richard Knight's butcher shop. Billy helped out at the shop, boarded at the Knight home, and often visited the family's Burro Mountain ranch. When Antrim went back to the mines, the boys stayed on at the Knight's to go to school. The house was home to Billy, and Mrs. Knight became almost a second mother to the boy.

Perhaps more than most boys, Billy had helped his ailing mother when she ran a boarding house. The familiarity he acquired with dishpan, broom and scrub board was learned of necessity, but stood him in good stead many times. His willingness to "help out" in their kitchens endeared him to overworked ranchers' wives who unanimously saw his good side.

Why did the boy leave Silver City? The letter writers declare that the stories quoted in most of the biographies are sheer nonsense or self-serving lies. They say he couldn't have killed some big brute for speaking insultingly to his mother for the good reason that his mother had died months before. Another

story tells that he killed a man who had wronged his sister Jeannie and then refused to marry her. There is no record that the Antrim brothers had a sister, whether wronged or not. The letters say there is no proof of violence or killing.

Something happened certainly, for the boy left town, hurrying to the protection of William Antrim, his stepfather. The man had probably tried as hard as most stepfathers do to care for his late wife's sons. Billy and Joe likely were as difficult as most teenagers can be. No doubt patience wore thin many times.

William Antrim told Dan McMillan, a fellow miner at Florida Flats, what had happened. "The dam' kid got into another scrape [unspecified] in town. I gave him what money I had in my pocket and told him to clear out and stay out."

So Billy got out. New Mexico Territory was a harsh and uncertain world for a youngster to face, but it didn't seem to have caused the boy much concern. Self-confident and fearless, if he ever looked back, except to miss his mother's love, it was not recorded. He walked, or possibly caught a ride on an ore wagon, the fifteen miles to the Burro Mountain ranch of the Knight family, his friends.

This was a pattern that was to be repeated many times in the boy's life. He always had loyal friends who were indeed friends in need. He was likable, known as "good company," and determined to "earn his keep" by doing whatever work needed to be done. He could cut firewood, mind the baby, wean the calves, help with the laundry, sweep the floor and, always wash the dishes.

Picture the future bad man up to his elbows in lukewarm soap suds. That was a scene often repeated in his life.

# Chapter Two

*Quien busca, halla.*
He who seeks, finds.

**W**hat does a skinny fourteen-year-old kid do when he is kicked out of the house with only the rattle of small change in his pocket?

Henry Antrim, still some time away from being known either as William Bonney or Billy the Kid, handled his dilemma in a manner he was to repeat over and over. Run away to friends. Do whatever work was needed "to pay his way." Then move on before his presence became an embarrassment or a danger to those who had befriended him.

So Billy "hedge-hopped" to the Knight's Burro mountain ranch. Hedge-hopping was an acceptable, if unorthodox,

# HEDGE - HOPPING

TEMPORARY LOAN OF A HORSE.
WHEN RELEASED AT OWNER'S BOUNDARY
LINE, THE MOUNT MEANDERS HOME.

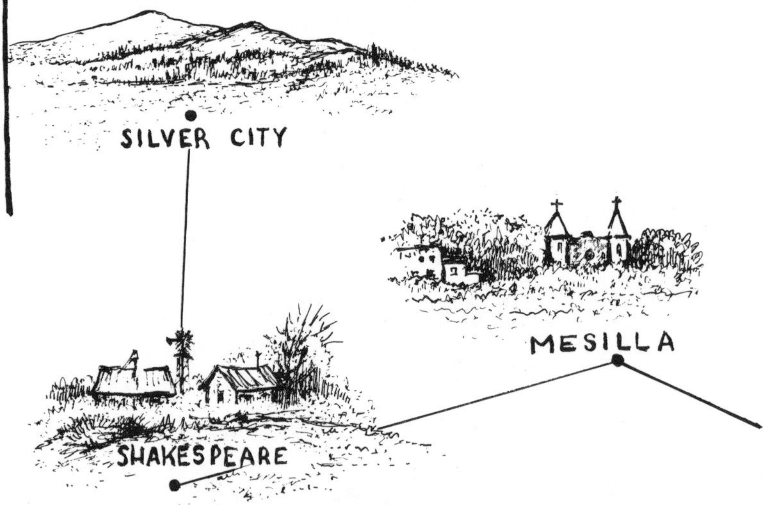

SILVER CITY

MESILLA

SHAKESPEARE

SEVEN RIVERS
(PECOS VALLEY)

GUADALUPE MOUNTAINS

method of getting from place to place by those who were, for one reason or another, afoot. A horse was caught, ridden until a line was reached that seemed to define the horse's home range, and then turned loose. Another horse was caught on the other side of the line and ridden in the direction the rider wished to go. It was a practice stoutly defended as borrowing and *not* stealing, for the horses eventually returned to their home ranges.

Billy stayed with the Knights for some time doing whatever work they found for him, either indoors or out. It was indoor most often for he never, on record, refused what was at the time dismissed as women's work.

That was another pattern repeated throughout his life. He cheerfully and ably "helped out" at the dishpan and washtub. Letter after letter told of the way Billy had worked beside the women doing the homey tasks necessary to keep a family fed and decently clothed, when neither was easy. "Billy understood," they wrote, "how hard it was to keep a family clean and clothed, darned and decent." And they loved him for his understanding and help. The enemies the boy made were never of the feminine gender.

He wandered in the area for some time, going from one mining camp to the next, doing anything that would help him earn his board and keep. He stayed for a few days in Ralston, or Grant, or Shakespeare. He was seen in Silver City now and then, a point letter writers made to prove he wasn't wanted for anything serious. He didn't seem to act like a fugitive or be worried about what the next day might bring.

From ranch to ranch he moved, staying as long as the work he could do held out. Then he moved on. He returned often to the Knight ranch, which was a station on the stage route between Silver City and the mining camps. He stood a good chance of being recognized by passengers if he was wanted, so if he did not wish to embarrass his loyal friends, it was time to move on.

Here legend branches out. His friends believe he went to Arizona Territory by the usual method of hedge-hopping. Others, not so lenient, describe how Billy and an 'accomplice' left Silver City with two Indians who rode good horses. The two arrived in Arizona with the horses and without the Indians. The letter writers want to know how a "scrawny kid" could have managed that.

Legend or not, the necessity for making a living remained. For the next two years the boy survived as a saddle tramp, working as a sheepherder, cowhand, farm worker and teamster. The letter writers say he had no part in the bloodthirsty adventures in Arizona and Mexico ascribed to him by later writers who had their reasons for portraying the boy as thoroughly bad and dangerous.

Boy he was. The men who hired him and trusted him with their property during that time doubted his statement of age. J.W. Smith (known as 'Sorghum') said, "The Kid came to my hay camp on the Gila asking for work. He said he was seventeen but he didn't look to me to be fourteen."

Drifting to Camp Grant, Arizona, the boy's education continued in the company of the men he encountered in the saloons and at the gaming tables. Always friendly and usually well-liked, the boy, who had grown enough to be called a young man, loafed and gambled and worked at whatever jobs he could find.

During the two years he worked as a cowboy, a teamster, a herder and in the post saw mill, he was usually in the company of men much older than he. It was natural that he was referred to as, "the Kid." He began at some time during this period to use the name William Bonney. From that it was an easy transition to "Billy the Kid."

He somehow acquired enough skill at cards to make a precarious living, so he stopped the dish washing — except as a friendly interchange — while he perfected another interest. He worked at marksmanship. A man who knew of the Arizona days wrote, "Billy was everlastingly popping off at targets. He must have spent every spare cent on ammunition then and he didn't do any different the rest of his days."

It is fact that Billy drove a log team from a timber camp to the Camp Grant saw mill for some time. What is doubtful is the story that he attempted to steal the team and wagon when he was laid off by the post quartermaster. The letter writers thought that tale, like some of the Silver City stories, was an embellishment added after Billy's outlaw years. One writer said, ". . .they blamed him for everything, just so it was bad enough."

The official record of his Arizona deeds began on August 17, 1877. Windy Cahill, a burly blacksmith at the post, had been nagging and bullying the boy for some time. One day tempers flared and slaps and blows were traded. Heavily outweighed, the boy was knocked down. As he dodged a kick, he rolled over and shot his tormentor. The blacksmith died the next day.

Billy was locked in the post guardhouse. A justice of the peace, who had witnessed the shooting, conducted the inquest. He found "that the killing was criminal and unjustified," a view that was not held by other onlookers. Billy was returned to jail but did not remain there very long. One night a sentry was heard to fire one or two shots at an "escaping prisoner." Pursuit was languid and an inquiry concerning which soldiers could have helped with the escape was inconclusive. All that was proved was that Billy always made friends in every situation.

He left the post on the fastest horse in the corrals, John Murphey's Cashew. This was a version of the time honored hedge-hopping. A week later a traveler came to the post leading Cashew and returned the horse to its owner, as he said the Kid had asked him to do.

Billy returned to his friends, the Knight family. On the Burro Mountain ranch he was welcome and safeguarded. He remained there, staying discreetly out of sight, for several weeks, but he refused to remain longer. When Billy told Mrs. Knight that he was leaving to go to the Mesilla Valley, she wept, but could not change his mind. She told him to take any horse from the corral as a gift. He made his farewells and rode away "on the scrubbiest animal of the lot."

# Chapter Three

*Lo cotrés no quita lo valiente.*

Valor is not found without courtesy.

The Rocky Arroyo Trail that led to the Heiskell Jones ranch near Seven Rivers, New Mexico, lived up to its name. Ma'am Jones, about to finish the family washing at the back door, watched with sympathy the traveler who came afoot. No wonder he was limping.

When she saw the slight youth stagger, she hurried toward him. "He's only a boy," she told herself. "And a half-dead boy at that!"

His boot soles had worn through and torn away. His feet were swollen and bleeding. Ma'am Jones half carried the slight boy to the bench beside the back door and set his punished feet into the still warm wash water she had been ready to pour out.

After his ruined boots were cut off she dried his feet and doctored them with grease and concern.

Billy told her about the great blunder that had brought him to such a state. He hadn't wanted to leave Mesilla for he had made friends there, but there was no work to be had. Coming from Eugene Van Patten's ranch, where he had been turned down for a job, he met Tom O'Keefe who had no better luck. The boys decided to move on to the Pecos Valley and continue their search for work at the ranches and settlements there.

Billy told Ma'am Jones they should have listened to the men of Mesilla, those veterans of Indian raids. "They told us to go to Lincoln by way of the Tularosa, Ruidoso and Hondo Valleys. 'Longer but less Apaches,' they said. But we knew better, of course," Billy said wryly. "We thought to save time and miles by a short cut across the Guadalupe Mountains."

A day into the rugged country, Billy had scrambled into a canyon to fill their canteens from the thread of water there, leaving Tom on the rim with the horses and gear. When the Indians struck, Billy could do nothing but dive into the shrubbery at the base of the canyon wall.

After a long silent time, he moved out until he could see the place where he had left Tom, but he saw nothing. The Indians had either killed or captured him and gone off with the horses, the bed rolls, guns and provisions.

Without food or weapons, and with little water, Billy had hidden by day and traveled by night. Half dead from starvation, thirst and exhaustion, he reached the Jones ranch. Ma'am Jones, called the 'Angel of the Pecos' because of her goodness, took Billy and cared for him until his feet were healed. By that time the homeless boy and the ranch woman had become fast friends. She mothered him as she did her nine sons. He on his part filled the place in her heart left empty and grieving since the death of her only daughter.

What really endeared the boy to Ma'am Jones was his willingness to go with her on regular visits to her daughter's grave.

On the way he gathered a handful of wild flowers to place beneath the wooden head marker, then he knelt beside the sorrowing mother in sympathetic silence. While she prayed and wept, he held her hand.

Billy limped around helping with the pots and pans and wash tubs and kept the wood box filled, as few men of his time would have done. When his feet healed, he helped with the outside work. There, Ma'am's son John and Billy became fast friends. Their friendship later survived the strain of being on opposite sides in the Lincoln County War, a conflict which caught them up in divided allegiances.

There was nothing for Billy on the ranch except make-work. He followed the continuing pattern of his life and left when his presence might have become a burden. When the time came to move on, Ma'am Jones wept and John Jones provided Billy with a horse.

He rode sixty miles up the Pecos Valley from Seven Rivers, exploring the countryside in his search for work. He reached South Springs Ranch feeling hopeful. The ranch was owned by John Chisum, the Cattle King, who needed many hands to herd the thousands of cattle wearing his Jingle Bob brand. But Billy was not hired. At a later time, Billy rode for Chisum as one of Chisum's warriors, a group acting more as a palace guard or personal army than as a clutch of cowboys. Billy argued later that he had not been paid for the services he rendered. The letter writers said the Cattle King was notoriously slow and reluctant to pay out money.

The smiling, good-looking Billy Bonney seemed to have made little impression on Chisum, but it was different with his niece Sallie. Her diary recorded considerable interest in the young visitor. She liked his cheerful, respectful manners and made opportunities to talk with him. Billy gave her small presents (duly noted in her diary) of an "Indian tobacco bag" and a "candi heart."

It is possible that Uncle John Chisum observed the mutual attraction. Perhaps that was the reason he found no work for the boy on his wide range. With no encouragement to stay, Billy's proud determination to accept no favors without repayment sent him riding. As he left Chisum's Jingle Bob range behind and turned toward the green valleys and blue mountains of the Lincoln country, he couldn't have known that he was going from the frying pan into the fire.

Happily for him it was some time before things heated up. He went from place to place among the small ranches, making friends wherever he stayed. As long as he could be persuaded to remain, he was welcome. Light hearted and companionable, he rode and worked and hunted with the menfolk, played with the children as if he were their own age, helped the wives with the cooking (often arriving with a quarter of beef, its origin never discussed), and danced with all the girls at every *baile* within riding distance.

The good side of the not-yet-bad man showed most clearly in his friendships. Certainly, he came to the remote ranches with everything in his favor. For the time and place, he was the perfect guest. He brought novelty and cheerfulness that brightened days that generally were both dull and dangerous. The people who called him friend recognized that the handsome laughing boy had a lurking devil in him, but with them he was just a good-natured imp. From his school days he was full of fun and mischief. "He made us laugh," they said of him. He joked and sang as he went cheerfully about the work that he shared with the men and women. One of them said, "That cheerful little gambler made the winter shorter and we hated to have him go, come spring."

But with the spring, the fire grew hot.

# Chapter Four

*Son ricos aquéllos quienes tienen amigos.*
Those who have friends are rich.

**H**ere, then, is a story of riches . . . .

The little boy had been sick and was supposed to be staying in bed. With one ear listening for anyone coming to check on him, he tiptoed along the hall of Pete Maxwell's big house. The door that usually stood half open was closed. Why?

Coming close he leaned against the door. Floor boards creaked . . . he heard a thud and a thump, followed by an annoyed mutter. That usually empty room wasn't empty.

He heard a soft laugh . . . the door he leaned against opened suddenly. Just as suddenly, he was pulled inside, and the door closed behind him.

The little boy stared up at the young man who clutched him. He saw a friendly grin and intent blue eyes under a cap of light brown hair. He saw ragged pants, feet in stockings, and in a corner, a pair of scuffed boots. None of that looked scary; he wasn't frightened.

"Why are you hiding in my Pa's storeroom?" the child demanded.

The young man put a finger to his lips. "It's a game," he whispered, "I want to see how long I can stay here without anyone knowing. Don't tell on me and I won't tell on you." He tweaked the little boy's ears in mock seriousness. "You're supposed to be staying in bed. I head Dulvena tell you so. Have you got something catching?"

"I don't think so. But Mama makes me stay in bed when she feels my forehead and it's hot." The little boy looked at the rumpled camp bed, a bucket, a water jar and a tin cup neighboring a plate smeared with egg and chili and drew the obvious conclusion. "Are you supposed to stay in bed, too? Because your forehead's hot?"

The young man dropped on all fours to be the child's height and held up his face. "Feel."

Giggling, the little boy felt the man's tanned forehead. "Down here you look like a horse. Horses don't get hot foreheads. Horses don't stay inside either. They're out where people can ride them."

"This horse needs to stay inside until dark, but he can give you a ride." He kicked back with one foot and managed to prance on knuckles and knees. "Come one! Have a ride!"

"Hang on, now!" the horse said with a nicker. "This is a bucking bronc!"

The 'horse' reared and sunfished, clomping around in the small space. The child, clinging to the young man's shirt and collar, shouted with laughter. After a few scampers the young man's knees protested. He put his head down, sliding the little boy to his shoulders. Then, holding the small hands, he stood up and galloped.

Around and around they went, the young man taking care that he bent low or turned sharply aside when they passed the open window at the far end of the room. But the noisy, laughing canter went on, all thought of quiet forgotten.

A tall man wearing a star and a gun, who came on the patio outside, glanced in as he passed. He smiled at the horse and rider galloping away from the window with the boy digging his heels in the horse's ribs.

It was nice of one of the hands to take time to amuse the young'un, Pat Garrett thought. Looked like he was getting over what it was that had kept him indoors. He glanced up at the sun and walked faster toward his mount. He was late getting on the trail to check out the report that Billy the Kid had been seen down on the Bonito.

Inside the room the 'horse' let the little boy slide over his head to land in a laughing heap on the rumpled bed. "Here we are, pal. Right back where we started from." He leaned over to give the boy a playful swat. "Thanks, *muchacho*. Pat might have looked a little closer if you hadn't been such a good bronc rider. Now you scoot back to bed before Dulvena wallops us both."

The lives of Billy the Kid and Pat Garrett were early and curiously intertwined. Billy had been working only a short time for Pete Maxwell in the sheep camps near Fort Sumner when he was approached by a tall stranger who said he badly needed a job. The fact that the stranger was practically in tatters emphasized that his need was real. Five-feet-seven-inch Billy loaned six-feet-four Pat Garrett his only other pair of trousers. They fit him "a little quick" but so-clothed, Pat Garrett could go to Pete Maxwell and be hired to work with the sheep as Billy did. When the friends met later, they were on opposite sides of the law.

That's a bad man? A young fellow who would loan his clothes to a stranger or with a price on his head, take a chance with his life to amuse a sick child?

Such stories, told by those who knew him, raise questions about the real William Bonney, known as Billy the Kid, the number one bad man of the pioneer West. In our reading of history, we tend to believe in two classes of those outside the law, Good Bad Men and Bad Bad Men. Our letter writers had no doubt about Billy.

"He was never mean," they declared. "He didn't even look mean."

The way he looked made first impressions favorable. He conformed to the accepted image of the Good Bad Man. He was young and personable. Slight and of medium height, his bold, yet pleasant manner, was said to mark him in a crowd. Wavy light brown hair, worn long, framed a smooth face dominated by expressive eyes that looked clearly blue, or gray, or smoky, mirroring his mood. Much has been made of protruding teeth that actually seem to have been only somewhat crowded in his small mouth, giving him a constant, slightly smiling expression. His build was athletic and his movements graceful. He had small hands and feet that made him deft and agile.

One eye-catching characteristic was his fastidious neatness. The scrawny boy in shabby, too-big clothes who hung around bars and studied the gambling tables in Silver City grew up as a saddle tramp, but didn't look like one. The few pictures show him in rumpled clothing with a hat squashed down on his head. "Billy didn't look like *that*," the letter writers said. "Not when he could help it." His hats were carefully tended and with a "go-to-hell" tilt. His boots were fitted and, by care, were clean.

When he rode to the available *bailes* (and that was whenever possible, for he loved to dance), he wore his best. That best was a black frock coat, dark trousers neatly tucked into his boot tops and a vest over a clean white shirt.

Where his clothes came from is a question. On one occasion we are told he gave his entire wardrobe to a needy friend, then went out and stole a replacement for himself. When he had money he was cheerfully generous. He bought shoes and coats for little kids, so presumably he outfitted himself as well.

He had a way with children and spent time with them when it was possible. His friends pointed out that dogs, too, liked him and concluded that such wouldn't be true of a Bad Bad Man. Billy, who could always take a joke on himself, would say that all dogs didn't know they *should* like him. As an example, he told of the time he came, wounded and hunted, to the door of a friend. His knocking went unanswered for the people inside did not recognize his voice and felt it prudent to bar the door to unknowns who came under cover of darkness. The dogs took their cue from their master and chased Billy up a tree. "And there I perched all night long like a jay bird on a limb," said New Mexico's most famous bad man.

The good side of the not-yet-bad man showed clearly and almost innocently in those days. He made friends everywhere he went. He played marbles with the kids in the ring behind Montaño's store in Lincoln, taking care that the big kids let the little kids win once in a while. He visited in and out of the houses of the *paisanos*, and was truly liked by the native New Mexicans for his fluent Spanish and his care for their dignity when the flood of aggressive new settlers endangered their way of life.

The letter writers insisted that he never approached a woman without his hat in his hand or spoke to one with less respect than he would have used to his own mother. One useful result was that Billy's sweet tooth was gratified by good cooks who fired up their ovens when they saw him coming. Addicted to *empañadas*, the small fruit pies (especially apple) that his friends made for him, Billy could usually keep his saddle bags filled. Always generous, he was seen returning to the sheep camp munching on one of the fruit-filled delicacies and handing out others to the children who ran after him. He took care to see that some were left for his friends, the herders. When the supply ran low, he might even part with the last pie while talking loudly about his greedy friends.

# Chapter Five

*Poco a poco se va lejos.*

Little by little one goes far.

He slipped through the door and stood close to the wall, looking back along the way he had come. He said over his shoulder without turning, "They're at the corner. . .be here in a few minutes. Hop into bed, you two."

The Mexican couple, who had sprung to their feet when he entered, stared in bewilderment. The young man was their friend *Billito*, but what was this about going to bed when it was barely dusk?

"I've got to hide," the young man said. "Where else?"

They followed his gaze around the small adobe room. A table, two chairs, corner fireplace, a pile of sheepskins. . . . They understood.

Minutes later three soldiers and a lieutenant pushed in without knocking, rifles at the ready. "Where is he? We know he came down here after he shot Bernstein on the Mescalero Apache Reservation. Where's he hiding?"

The man on the floor pulled the sheepskin up to his chin. "*Quién es, senor? Mis esposa y me en la cama.*"

"Kind of early, ain't you?" The lieutenant leered and one of the soldiers snickered.

The sheepskins humped and straightened; the wife's face turned red and she covered her embarrassment with her hands.

The lieutenant took a last look at the empty room. "I can see you ain't got the Kid hid in here. If you see him, you'd better turn him in. They got trouble at the Agency with that fellow from Washington nosing around counting rations. That's likely why Bernstein got shot."

The young woman sat up. "You can't blame *Billito* for that. . . ."

The sheep skins wiggled and humped. With a gasp, the wife disappeared under them.

The sheep skins and the adobe room were quiet for a few minutes after the door slammed behind the soldiers. Then things came apart in giggles and laughing whispers.

"*Billito* pinched me!"

"*Billito* pulled my toes!"

The Kid dared danger like a moth flickering around a candle flame. He was the very symbol of youth dancing on a precipice. Much of his illegal activity was adolescent defiance of authority and exposure of the hypocrisy and dishonesty of the ruling class that he came in contact with. He was fearless and loved taking chances. Adding fun to the danger made it even more to his liking.

Stories told in the letters and interviews illustrated his light-heartedness. He only surrendered to Pat Garrett at Stinking Springs after a joking attempt to bargain for fire and food. Jailed then at Las Vegas, he talked cheerfully with the curious who came to stare while he waited for the train that would take him to Santa Fe and prison. "What's the good of looking on the dark side of everything?" he asked. "The joke's on me this time."

As the train pulled out taking him to a certain death sentence, he tipped his hat to the crowd and invited them to come see him at his new address. In a short time, a change of venue moved his trial to Mesilla where he felt he would get only a perfunctory defense. When the train reached Las Cruces, the Kid sat shackled to his seat waiting to be taken to Mesilla. A crowd of the curious ran alongside peering in the windows at the passengers. They asked excited questions, "Which one is Billy the Kid? Where's the Kid?"

Billy stood up and laid his hand on the head of Judge Ira Leonard, his appointed counsel who sat beside him. "Here he is!" he shouted. "Here's the bad man!"

If the people of Mesilla could have managed it, Billy would have gone free from charges they felt made him a scapegoat for crimes he hadn't committed, or had only a part in. "Did the bullet that killed Sheriff Brady have Billy's name on it?" his friends asked. "How about those other men who shot the lawman at the same time?"

They received no answers to their questions and were obliged to show their sympathy for their friend by bringing him food and visiting through the bars of the village jail. Each morning a small boy brought a pint of fresh milk and was always paid five cents for his trouble. Billy's sweet tooth was fed with gifts of candy, his favorite pies and chewing gum. If one can be said to be entertained in jail, he was.

When he was sentenced to hang for the murder of Sheriff Brady and transferred to confinement on the top floor of the courthouse at Lincoln, the Kid's good humor seemed constant. "Perhaps he knew he wasn't born to be hung," one writer said.

His belief in his destiny was apparent when he was visited by a young woman who had watched Billy play with her children when he rode by the saw mill where they lived. One of Billy's guards, who knew that the young woman liked the Kid, took delight in inviting her to the hanging. As she turned away with tears in her eyes, Billy said gently, "They can't hang me if I'm not there, can they?"

Like the men he rode with, the Kid relished practical jokes. Most of the jokes were simple and crude, often involving his dexterity with guns. He sometimes rode up beside his victim, snatched off his hat and threw it into the air. Before the hat fell to the ground he had riddled it with bullets. (Apparently none of the writers who found this amusing had been owners of the hats.) Or he might ask a friend which hat he fancied as they approached a group. When one was pointed out, Billy would smilingly take it from the man who wore it and bestow it on his friend, all without a word of explanation.

One time the record showed that Billy terrified an innocent peddler by asking him if he liked to dance. When the man replied that he wasn't good at dancing, Billy said he could teach him how to improve. As he shot off the heels off the peddler's boots, the man proved to be a quick study, leaping and hopping as the bystanders jeered. As the smoke cleared away, the peddler was applauded as a good sport.

When he had once thrown the men around a campfire into a panic by tossing a handful of ammunition into the flames to explode, they planned to startle him by the same means. But the joke failed. Billy reached for his guns and fell into a position of defense ready for what might happen. "He never turned a hair," the disappointed jokers said.

He had a humorous turn of speech that was remembered by some of the writers. There was the time he was asked why he was riding such a poor horse, something he seldom did. "Well, I'll tell you," Billy said, "if I had one just like him, I'd ride the other one."

Another time the campfire talk concerned the surprising news that a little scrawny cowpuncher they all knew had married a woman three times his size. Billy explained it, "I think the poor devil had seen so many starved, gaunt cows he appreciated one that had a little flesh on her."

# Chapter Six

*Adiós al mundo.*
Goodbye, the world.

**T**he young man moved his chair nearer the lamp and took up his pen again. He began to write. He may have remembered, for he had been considered a good student at school in Silver City, a motto at the top of a page in the penmanship manual: "The pen is mightier than the sword." He hoped it was true.

> *To His Excellency the Governor Lew Wallace*
> *Dear Sir:*
>
> *I have heard that you will give $1,000 for my body which I understand means alive as a witness against those who murdered Wm. Chapman. If it*

> *was so that I could appear in court I could give the*
> *desired information but I have an indictment*
> *against me for things that happened in the last*
> *Lincoln County War and am afraid to give up*
> *because my enemies would kill me.*

He laid the pen down and swiped absently at the moth that circled the flame. Maybe that was what he was doing, too . . . tempting fate. But he had believed the governor when the two had met secretly. He was to trade testimony against Jesse Evans, William Campbell and James Dolan, and yes, even against Colonel A. M. Dudley, for a pardon from the governor. Although the actual whereabouts of this letter Billy wrote to the governor is unknown, it may be among those recently donated to the Lincoln County Heritage Foundation by Governor Wallace's descendants.

He drew a long breath that was almost a sigh and took up the pen again. He must finish the letter . . . .

*I have no wish to fight anymore.*

What the Kid didn't realize and what Governor Wallace didn't know was that the Santa Fe Ring—the judge and the district attorney—had no intention of permitting that testimony. As time passed, the governor came to understand the official position. His first exchanges with Billy had been sympathetic, but his attitude eventually changed, until he would write with sarcasm:

> *. . . the Kid is an object of tender regard here (Lin-*
> *coln). I heard singing and music the other night;*
> *going to the door I found minstrels of the village*
> *actually serenading the 'fellow' in his prison.*

It was obvious to the letter writers that the governor didn't take the Kid seriously. From Billy's school days, people in power had failed to recognize the quality of his leadership.

Almost always the youngest in any group, he was credited with proposing many things, from practical jokes to a plan for stopping the Lincoln County War before it began. "And," said the writers stoutly, "some of his plans were good."

They held the opinion that had Billy's appeal to Governor Lew Wallace been taken seriously, the bad man would have lived to become a man of substance and integrity. They didn't blame the governor too much. He was busy, they knew, with his classic best-seller *Ben Hur: A Tale of the Christ*, but they thought he was a better writer than a keeper of promises.

Men were measured in those stern old times by an unwritten, but definite, code. Anglos and Hispanics, natives and in-coming settlers alike understood that it was easy enough for men to go wrong because there was no restraining body of public opinion. Surely, they saw and experienced, the destructive power of the harsh environment on the human character. There was little law, so men of integrity governed themselves by what they believed to be right.

They lived and died by the belief that a man upheld the strengths of courage, loyalty, steadfastness, forbearance toward the weak, clannishness, resolution to stay out of other people's business, no expectation that other men should right one's wrongs, and far from being the last on the list, cheerful dignity under difficulties.

Lest the code seem to look only on the sunny side (perhaps that of the angels), it was underlaid with the oldest code of all, that of an 'eye for an eye and a tooth for a tooth.' Kindness and generosity coexisted with hatred and revenge. Billy was no different from his peers in believing that misdeeds should exact their payment. Taking the law (largely absent) in one's own hands was the action of a 'man.'

The letter writers thought the Kid stood up well under the light of the unwritten code. They didn't excuse his misdeeds, but in a manner startlingly like those held by many today, they "understood his motives." Leaving the indisputable hard facts to the historians, consider how legend rates the Kid by the code.

His courage seems unchallenged. One wrote of him as, "the bravest man I had ever know." His friends believed he "never ran from a fight or quit before he was licked," but allowed that "to leave when hopelessly outclassed only made sense, and Billy was no fool."

Still less to be questioned was his loyalty. Billy believed, and certainly demonstrated, that a man stood by his friends, right or wrong, win or lose. Wisdom, or even a little of the frontier's horse sense, would have advised that he back out of the tragic events that led to and followed the Lincoln County War. But he chose to stay with his friends.

That he benefited by his loyalty became abundantly certain when a price, placed on his head, made him fair game for the bounty hunters. Five hundred dollars, and later a thousand, was a fortune. Most of Billy's friends would not see that much money in a lifetime. But he moved among them with no fear of betrayal. Along the Hondo and the Bonito, the Peñasco and the Pecos, the Ruidoso and the Rio Grande, the little people sheltered and fed and lied for him, unanimously.

The dark code that commanded each man to right his own wrongs led the Kid straight to his own death. Billy had felt a young man's admiration for the Englishman John Henry Tunstall who had, in Billy's words, "given him his first real job," outfitted him with horse and gear and "made me the first present I ever had, of a rifle." To avenge his friend's murder became the fatal determination that cost Billy his own life.

Measured by the standards of his time, and compared with his fellows outside the law, the letter writers never doubted that Billy was a Good Bad Man. They did not particularly recognize that he — as they themselves — had been caught up in a process of history that invariably follows the opening of a frontier. He "strayed," they said, into the violence of the times and was caught up in a vicious struggle between two factions. Murder between herdsmen and tillers of the soil was as old as Cain and Abel. The fight for wealth and power didn't come to an end with the Territorial days.

That Billy had his day in court and the defense to which today every man is entitled is debatable. From the handed-down opinions and memories of a hundred years, there seems much admissible evidence to prove there was indeed a good side to New Mexico's best known bad man.

# Testimony

*Mas ven cuatro ojos dos.*
Four eyes are more than two.

**H**ere, in their own words, are quotations from the letters and interviews collected by the writer and the artist. These are the threads from which our sampler of the good side of a bad man was stitched.

"I am near eighty years old but so far I have all my buttons and will tell you what I know."

"It's about time someone told some of the truth about the Kid."

"I found the Kid a likable youngster, but saw that he would not be crossed. . . ."

"In the main the outlaws were easy going, likable young fellows."

"My grandfather told stories of living one winter in a cabin with a happy-go-lucky gambler."

"He was in many ways a good boy . . . not half as bad as many others of his time."

"He was about the same as most boys of his age."

"Billy was a good example. He understood that being clean and polite could be manly. He knew it was hard for the women to keep a family washed and combed, darned and decent."

"If there was a clean white shirt in the crowd it was on Billy's back."

"Few of them [incoming settlers] respected our rights or our dignity as Billy did."

"He was good to my people," said a *viejo* who spoke no English. "And during the early days many of the *gringos* were not. Some of them looked on my people as an inferior race."

This said in musical Spanish, "I cannot help thinking softly of him."

"My grandfather came on Billy butchering a calf in plain sight. He cut off a pound or so of the meat for himself, then told my grandfather with a ferocious frown, 'Now you take the rest of this home to that pack of hungry kids at your *casa* and if you talk about this, when I come back by, you won't be herding any more cows!"

"When he drove cattle through the village, somehow one cow would break away from the herd every time. Now *Billito* can't leave the herd to ride out and turn one ol' cow, can he? Certainly not! So Bang! Bang! Bang! He shoot him and we all make fiesta!"

"Uncle and Billy both knew the badge-toting bounty hunters would soon come riding by, so Billy moved on."

"Grandma said that when Billy had been there she wouldn't have to cut wood for a long time. . . . Grandpa said, when the

Kid rode up he knew he would have good help for as along as Billy would stay."

"There are none of God's creatures more quick to sense those they may trust than children and dogs. Billy loved them both and they loved him."

"He helped to bring a winter's load of wood for a family who couldn't get it for themselves. I knew him to ride to the home of a destitute family with a sack of food thrown over his saddle. Not to offend, he laughed and asked the lady to prepare a meal for him as a great favor. Then he rides away, grateful, leaving a bunch of food behind."

"He was the bravest man I ever knew."

"He never ran from a fight . . . to get out when he was hopelessly outclassed only made good sense."

"What if he didn't wait for the other man to make the first move? Billy was no fool."

"He was too sensible to be foolhardy, but he never backed down."

"Billy strayed into the fight and there was no one to save him."

"He was out of favor with Chisum and Catron, the two at the top."

". . . he felt tricked by Governor Lew Wallace."

"Billy was chased by the Texas ranchers' drunken crews who vandalized the Mexican plazas and sheep camps worse than the Comancheros."

"The solid evidence gives him no more than eight killed."

"The Kid got a bad shake and was made a convenient scapegoat."

"Thank you for what you are doing for the state's greatest gun fighter. After all he can't speak for himself. Our so-called law fixed that."

"We never doubted that a man had a right to take up for himself and fight for his rights and property."

". . . acted right according to his rights."

". . . if the little guy wanted to live and keep what he had worked for, he kept his mouth shut."

"The Kid was the bravest man I ever knew and I have known many brave men. I do not believe he knew the meaning of fear. When faced with danger, he was always calm."

". . . he maybe had more pluck than brains."

"I've heard some weird stories about Billy the Kid, none of which fit what I have come to know of him and his times . . . I don't think he was a blood thirsty killer . . . , just an ordinary young person who had to grow up at an early age. He was befriended by John Tunstall and, when Tunstall was murdered, he went after the ones he thought did it, one after the other, according to the code of the West."

"I am not clear as to why it was necessary to ambush him, but after all, the people who had wanted Tunstall out of the way were still powerful in the area."

"If Tunstall had lived, the Kid, under his guidance, would have become a valuable citizen, for he was remarkable, far above the average young men of the times. He had the makings of a fine man."

"Billy got away leisurely [after escaping from the Court House jail]. It was kinda' awkward mounting a horse with a shackle on one ankle and a chain hanging − he tucked that in his belt. Someone could have jumped him easily. They didn't want to."

"Poor boy, he never came back to our house. The next time I saw him he was a prisoner guarded by Bell and Olinger."

"Billy and his gang were blamed for much of the thieving and, while often guilty, I am sure they were charged for many a loss due to other gangs having their headquarters at the booming town of White Oaks or Fort Sumner and also at Seven Rivers."

"When it came to a death struggle, the mountain people were not about to side with the group that looked down on them and gave them a bad name."

"The men who rode with the Kid and got away were not smarter than he was. He could figure the odds as well as they. They disappeared from the Territory and the sight of history. Several were [later] found and located as surprisingly prosperous and respectable citizens! Why did the Kid stay? Because he loved New Mexico."

The writer and the artist rest their case.

# Epilogue

*Bueno mas tarde que nunca.*
Better Late Than Never.

**B**illy the Kid, New Mexico's legendary outlaw, has never had any luck with governors. Not a hundred years ago; not a hundred years later.

General Lew Wallace, Governor of the Territory of New Mexico, met with the fugitive Billy and exchanged promises that, hopefully, would bring Billy in to testify against a known murderer while his own safety was assured. The Kid's letters [many preserved in the Museum at Lincoln, New Mexico], when compared with Governor Lew Wallace's statements, suggest His Excellency, preoccupied with his best seller novel, *Ben Hur: A Tale of the Christ*, was a better author than a keeper of promises.

Latter day governors may understandably grow weary of New Mexico's best-known citizen. William Bonney, internationally known as Billy the Kid, has been immortalized in every conceivable media: books, plays, movies, pageants and ballets, popular songs and folk lore, researched minutely by amateur and professional historians, studied by learned seminars and featured in magazine articles and newspaper stories that total many thousands of words.

The governors have periodically been confronted with old citizens, apparently risen from the grave to prove they are Billy, not shot by Pat Garrett, and requesting pardons. Add to all that, a stream of tourists wanting to know all about him and where they can buy T-shirts. Governors can be forgiven if they sometimes wish that New Mexico's best-known citizen would quietly fade into history.

One day in late March of a recent year, the author and illustrator of this book you are reading, believing that they had presented reasonable proof of "the good side of a bad man," wrote a letter to the Governor. Remembering that Billy liked a practical joke, the writers timed their letter to arrive near April First. The letter went like this:

> *Your Excellency, Dear Sir:*
>
> *This letter accompanies a copy of <u>Billy the Kid:</u> <u>The Good Side of a Bad Man</u> which Marquita Peterson, Linda Harris and I, Lee Priestley, hope you will enjoy reading.*
>
> *Please, Sir, before you say, "Not another book about Billy the Kid!" and toss it in the wastebasket, will you stay with us a little longer? We believe this, perhaps the last unexamined aspect of the life and legend of New Mexico's best known citizen explains why he is still remembered more than a hundred years after his death. Our legendary bad man had a good side.*

*We aren't foolish enough to deny that William Bonney lived and died outside the law. We know that he took a casual attitude toward other people's property (particularly the four-legged, portable sort) and that he shot a few citizens, some declared to be of little loss to the Territory. We do think we have shown that he was never mean.*

*We believe it has been shown that he became a scapegoat, caught between powerful political and commercial interests. When he tried to escape from a tightening trap, his efforts to live on the right side of the law were rebuffed by prominent citizens whose broken promises do not adorn their careers.*

*Jailed on shaky evidence for his role in the April First, 1878, shooting death of Lincoln County Sheriff William Brady, he was indifferently defended and sentenced to hang. When he escaped (we don't forget nor excuse that he killed his guards) he became a fugitive with a five-hundred dollar price on his head, but he could range the Territory in safety, confident that he would not be betrayed. Finally, a bullet fired in the dark ended his short turbulent life.*

*Without condoning what he did, we would point out that if he came to trial today with our profusion of civil rights, public defenders, continuances, appeals, plea bargains and other legal maneuvers, we doubt that he would ever go to jail. Governor, Sir, if there is such a thing as a posthumous pardon, isn't Billy the Kid eligible for one?*

*On the practical side, such a pardon would enhance the legend and make The Kid an even greater tourist attraction. And, just think what it would do for the T-shirt business!*

> *Your Excellency, for the above reasons we ask*
> *your compassion and pardon for Billy the Kid, New*
> *Mexico's best known citizen.*
>
> *Respectfully, etc.*
> *The Letter Writers*

Those letter writers do not know exactly who read or considered their letter, so they were astonished to receive a reply from the Pardon and Extradition Board. In a somewhat impatient tone, they were informed that the requested pardon was impossible because (a) there was no time to consider it since there were hundreds of living persons with pending cases, and (b) because the case would be more than a hundred and twenty years old, a full investigation of the facts would be impossible since any witnesses would be dead.

The letter writers gasped, then they chuckled. Their tongue-in-cheek request for a pardon for Billy the Kid had been taken seriously, had become a practical joke for April Fool's Day that would have tickled the Kid himself. The letter writers would have left it there, but a reporter caught it when looking for a story on a dull day. We hurriedly wrote another letter to the Governor's office apologizing for any misunderstanding or embarrassment that our mild joke might have caused.

That was all we had time for. Our phones rang constantly, our door bells chimed, interviewers crowded the doorsteps. We found ourselves appearing somewhat uneasily on local and national news and talk shows on radio and TV, coast-to-coast. We tried to answer questions that showed more people knew about Billy the Kid than were sure that New Mexico was actually within the borders of the United States. Some of the better questions came one surprising day when we found ourselves taking part in a talk show from Adelaide, Australia.

Only a small pebble had been tossed in a big pond, but the resulting ripples have been persistent and surprising. New

Mexico's legendary bad man is known to people half way around the world who, whether we like it or not, are totally unaware and indifferent to the more worthy personages of the time. Most of the people who were interested in Billy considered him a Good Bad Man rather than a Bad Bad Man, but they did know of him.

Who can doubt that William Bonney, better known as Billy the Kid, is New Mexico's best-known citizen?

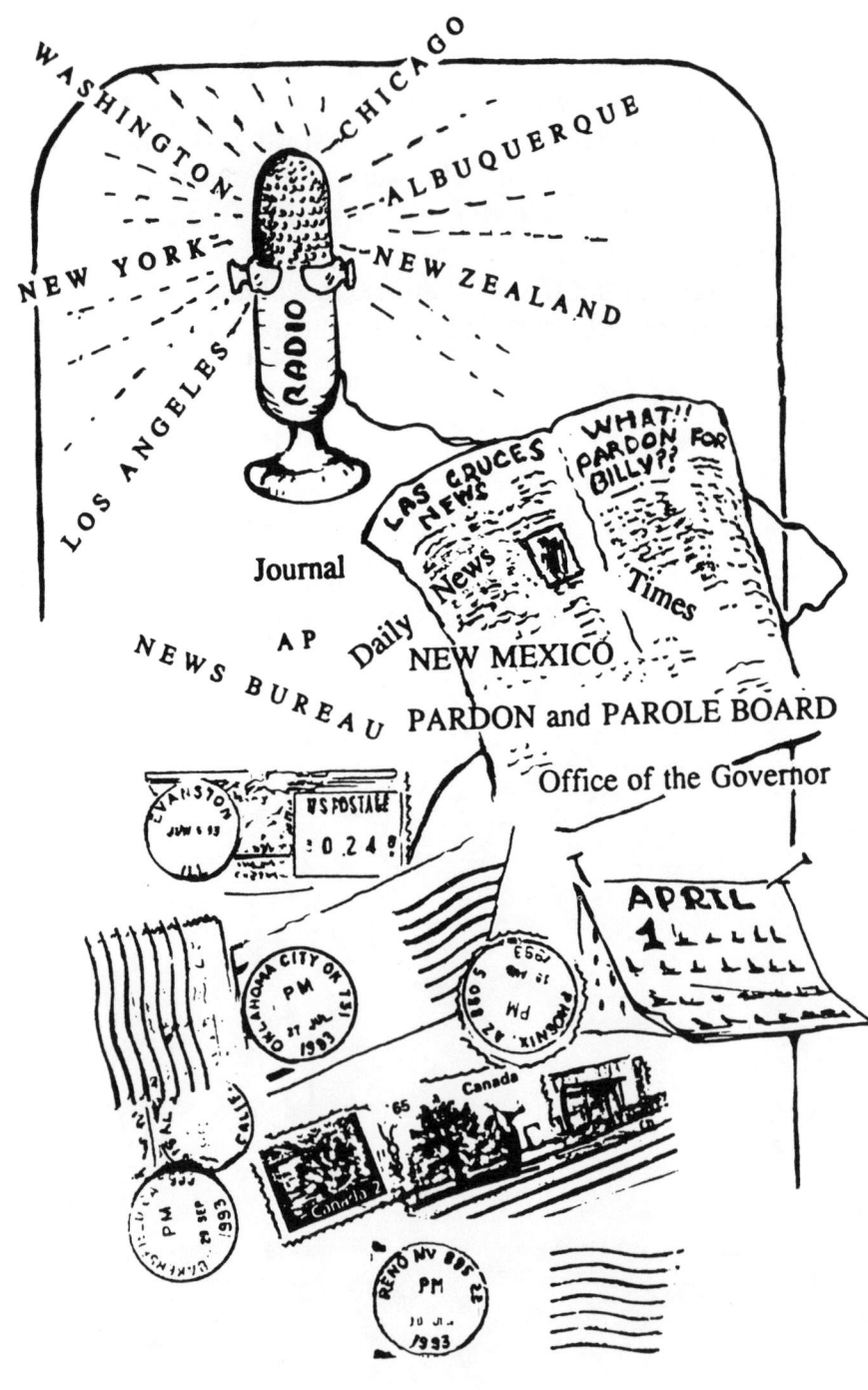

# INDEX

**Author Lee Priestley** was born in Kansas, educated in Oklahoma, and resided for many years in Louisiana and New Mexico. She is the author of numerous novels and picture books and more than a thousand short stories. Much of her work, like *The Good Side of a Bad Man*, has southwestern settings and characters.

She lives in Las Cruces, New Mexico, and has taught creative writing at the University of Oklahoma and New Mexico State University. Her most recent books are *Shalam: Utopia on the Rio Grande*, which traces the creation and collapse of Shalam Colony, a nineteenth century noble experiment in which found-lings, orphans, and neglected children were reared in a communal society, and *Journeys of Faith*. *Journeys of Faith* is the story of Preacher Lewis, the Episcopal missionary who, for half a century, served a parish of 28,000 square miles along the Rio Grande.

**Artist Marquita Peterson** is a native New Mexican who has studied art in Texas, Oregon and Idaho. Her works in oil, water color and ink are in private and corporate collections throughout the country.

She teaches art classes in oil, watercolor and creative drawing in Albuquerque, New Mexico, where she now makes her home. Her current emphasis is on historical southwestern subjects. Her *Southwest Legacies* series of sepia ink drawings is reconstructed from tintypes and archival photos from the Lincoln County War era.